Passport to Travel Security

Passport to travel Security

A guide to staying safe when travelling overseas

David Harding

<Security Management Solutions>
<2013>

Passport to Travel Security

First Printing: <2013>

ISBN <978-1-291-59203-0>

<Security Management Solutions>
<331 Messingham Road>
<Bottesford>, <North Lincolnshire> <DN17 2QZ>
www.<securitymanagementsolutions>.co.uk

Contents

Acknowledgements

To the many places I have visited and the people I have met along the way. Thank you.

Without your influence, sometimes good, sometimes not so good, this book would not have been possible.

Travelling to new countries, experiencing new cultures and lifestyles has been and continues to be a valuable education.

Introduction

The world is an uncertain place. Even a casual glance at world news over recent years will have shown images of travellers being caught up in violent incidents, such as rape, robbery, murder, kidnapping, terrorist attacks or even entire countries descending into revolution or civil war. Standards of accommodation, facilities, crime, sanitation, health & safety, driving standards and cultural differences can differ greatly from what you are used to in your home country and be a great surprise to the uninformed business or leisure traveller.

Now more than ever, travellers (especially business travellers) need to be aware of security threats and take steps to ensure their safety. Investing just a little time in careful planning before you travel can protect you and your belongings and reduce the chances of becoming a victim of crime or personal injury. This publication seeks to help you do just that.

Chapter 1: Preparing to travel

Being properly prepared and having the right information before you even start to travel can help you avoid trouble and know what to do if you encounter any problems. When planning your trip, consider the following.

The UK (and US) government provides comprehensive travel advice for almost any country you may be likely to visit. This will give you advice on issues such as crime, terrorism, health and local customs, as well as highlight if there are any specific areas of the country which should be avoided, or which might need special permits or permissions from the local government in order to visit. It will also provide contact details of Embassy offices which can help you if you find yourself in trouble.

Check out their websites as part of your planning process at "www.gov.uk/foreign-travel-advice" or "www.travel.state.gov/travel".

Make a clear and concise itinerary of your trip, which includes names and contact details of the places and people you are going to visit. This should include methods of travel, such as flights, car hire information, airport transfer or taxi information. If you are going to be driving, check what licence & insurance you need. If you will be using taxis, get recommendations on company names and estimates of their rates for your journeys. It should also include details of where you will be staying, along with contact details and written confirmation of your accommodation booking. Make sure that someone else in the family or at work knows your itinerary, so they can alert someone if you run into trouble or "go missing".

Check carefully that some of the things you take for granted "at home" will actually work for you while you are travelling. Consider things such as – Is your passport valid, do you need a visa and are there enough "blank" pages in your passport for all of the visas or stamps you may need? Is your driving licence valid for the country you will be travelling in? Are your medical vaccinations up to date and do you need any new ones?

Will your mobile telephone work in the country you are travelling to and is it allowed to take it there (some countries do not allow encrypted phones such as "Blackberry's").

Will you be able to use your Debit or Credit Cards in that country (check with the hotel at your destination and don't forget to inform your bank you are travelling)? How much cash will you need for the trip and in what currency? Can you get that currency at home or only when you arrive there and if so, where will you get it from?

How easy will it be to communicate with "locals" in the country you are travelling to (How widely is your own language spoken there)? Do you have travel and medical insurance and will it cover you for all of the places you will be travelling to?

Make photocopies of your essential identity and travel documents, along with other "essential" information such as hotel bookings, car hire agreements, driving licence, insurance policies, bank card numbers (not PINs) and medical certificates.

Make a list of and pre-program into your mobile phone, all of the important contact numbers for your trip, including your next of kin, people you intend to meet while travelling, airline or travel organiser, hotel, taxi company, medical & travel insurance company, your bank "lost card" emergency number and the contact telephone number of your Embassy in the country you will be visiting.

It is often useful to take some "emergency" cash in low denomination US Dollar bills. These are widely accepted in other countries and will be a useful "back up" if things go wrong. Only take unmarked, good quality notes, as currency exchangers overseas will not accept heavily used or marked notes.

Pack carefully and in advance, so that you do not risk "forgetting" something later. In addition to suitable clothing for the local culture or climate, you might want to consider things such as a torch (in some countries the electricity supply can be very unstable), a door wedge (some hotels may not have security/privacy bolts or chains on room doors), basic medicines for headaches or stomach problems,

prescription medicines (take the prescription with you),
spare glasses/contact lenses, sanitary towels, tourist maps, notebook & pen, mobile telephone charger & spare battery etc. All bags should be labelled, but avoid using names and full addresses, rather use only a Post Code & telephone number. Bright coloured labels, tags or luggage straps will help you quickly identify your hold luggage at the baggage carousel.

Try to avoid using airline "gold card" luggage tags, as these could make your baggage "stand out" as being from a more affluent traveller and therefore more attractive to thieves.

Don't invite criminals into your home. The internet is a great tool, but it can also work against you. Criminals are always on the lookout for opportunity, so don't announce your travel plans "to the world" on social media sites such as Facebook. If you must "post" whilst travelling, be sure to ensure that your audience will be restricted to friends and family only - check the security settings on your social media sites reflect this.

Finally, don't forget to check that everything at

home is safe and secure before setting off on your trip, so that it will be in the same condition when you get back. Ask a friend or family member to check on your home periodically.

Chapter 2: Airports & Transit

Security checkpoints and airport departure & arrivals areas are popular locations for theft and scams. Be sure not to leave expensive items on top of your carry-on belongings when they go through airport security screening and watch them carefully as they do so. Carry your passport and flight ticket through the screening arch, clearly visible in your hand. Always be courteous with airport screening staff, no matter how they are treating you. You do not want to be delayed by additional screening processes, just because you lost your patience!

Restaurants and restrooms are also high crime areas. Laptop computers, other electronic gear, and personal items are extremely vulnerable to theft at airports and other busy, crowded areas. Thieves are experts at exploiting split-second opportunities to relieve you of your expensive business and personal items and will gladly do so, if you give them the chance. Never leave unattended personal items on tables or outside restroom stalls. Not only do you run the risk of them being stolen, but you also run the risk of causing a security alert!

Be careful when using free wifi at airports, as they provide great opportunities for criminals to intercept data or gain access into your computer or smart phone. Similarly, if you use shared computers in airports or hotels, be sure not to access sensitive sites, such as your bank or shopping accounts. You don't know how data is stored or accessed on these machines and you could leave yourself wide open for others to access your accounts. When you're finished, be sure to "log off" properly and clear the browser cache.

Be wary of people approaching you with offers to "help" you in finding ticket offices, currency exchange offices, car hire desks, taxis or helping you with your baggage. These are frequent ploys of criminals looking to steal your things or to ask you to pay later for their "services". Politely decline any such offers and find the official airport information desk to ask for assistance.

Carry all important documents or papers with you at all times throughout your journey.

Be aware of size and weight limits, and how many bags are permitted for carry-on. Carry-on limits vary among airlines. You do not want to get unexpectedly separated from your carry-on luggage, just as your about to board the flight. Especially if it contains all of your important documents or expensive items! Wherever possible, try to take direct flights. Flight connections carry a higher risk of losing your luggage and if there are problems with the connecting flight, you may be stuck in the airport for a long time, particularly if you don't have a visa for that country.

Never carry a bag or package for anyone else. They could contain drugs, contraband or other dangerous materials and the "excuse" that they belong to someone else will not be accepted or used in your defence at any subsequent criminal action against you.

On flights, try to be seated near (or next to) an emergency exit. If this is not possible, be sure to check where the nearest one is to your seat. The chances of needing to use it may be small, but why leave such an important thing as your route out of an emergency to chance?

Limit your conversations about your personal or business life to the bare minimum, even with colleagues, as you do not know who is sitting nearby. Also, be wary of "shoulder surfing" if you need to use your laptop during the flight.

Try to avoid alcohol on the flight. The smell of it on your breath may draw unwanted attention to you from customs or immigration officials on arrival at your destination, especially if the use of alcohol is "frowned upon" in that country. Take time during the flight to check with the flight attendants as to what the arrivals procedure is, including any customs or immigration form requirements and the process (and location of the office) for obtaining your visa (if you don't already have one).

Chapter 3: On arrival

Airports are crowded and busy places at the best of times. None more so than the "arrivals" experience and especially if you have never visited that particular airport (or country) before. Formal procedures for immigration and customs clearance may not be obvious, so take the time to check (before arrival if possible) that you know where to go and what to do.

Be aware of arrivals procedures such as a requirement to keep landing cards, customs forms etc for use on your departure journey. Also be aware of what may or may not be taken out of the country on your return journey. Some countries have strict rules about how much money can be taken out of the country.

Only use authorised outlets to exchange money or buy airline tickets. Do not use "black market" currency dealers, no matter how tempting the exchange rates might be. You run the risk not only of being cheated or robbed, but also of being arrested or imprisoned.

Use only legitimate taxis (cars with logo's, roof lights, and meters) for all journeys during you trip. It is always preferable to have organised this in advance with your contacts in the country or through the hotel. If not, then ask at the airport information desk for advice. Don't accept offers of shared taxis (common ploy used by criminals to target travellers) and always agree the taxi fare (and in what currency) before leaving the airport.

Be wary of people holding up signboards that display only the name of the hotel. Ask them to confirm the name of the person (don't give them this information yourself) they are meeting, before assuming it is you and that they are a "genuine" representative of the hotel.

Be wary of taxi drivers who seem to take too much interest in who you are, where you're from and what you will be doing during your visit. Limit your conversation to general pleasantries.

It's often useful to time journeys from the airport to the hotel (making allowances for time of day or weather conditions), so that you can properly plan for return journeys at the end of your trip.

Stay alert throughout the journey. The trip to and from the airport is usually the one which carries the highest risk, not just from criminals, but also in terms of driving standards and road conditions.

Chapter 4: At the hotel

On first arrival at your hotel, you should confirm or request a number of things before leaving the reception desk. Much may depend on the nature of your visit, but in terms of personal safety and security you should consider the following:

Confirm the hotel has registered your stay in accordance with any local government requirements, such as registering with the police or other security agencies. Ask that they take a copy of your passport, rather than holding onto the original document for any registration formalities they may need to complete.

Confirm your room facilities, the duration of your stay and how they will be charging you for this (specifically ask if you are paying by "card" that they accept this). When confirming your room, ask about security features, such as door viewers, chains & bolts. Ground floor rooms facing the outside, especially those

facing car parks or roads, are the easiest targets for break-ins.
Ask for a room on the second floor or above, but no higher than the sixth floor, as many fire departments in foreign countries do not have ladders or other equipment needed to rescue people above the sixth floor.

If you will be using taxis, ask the hotel for contact details of reputable companies. If you do not already have a local map, ask the hotel for one. Also ask about locations of ATM machines, currency exchanges and any other facilities you may need during your trip. Before leaving the reception desk, make sure you get a few of their business cards, match books or anything else small enough to fit in your wallet/pocket that has the name of the hotel on it in the local language. You may need this to get back to the hotel if the taxi drivers do not speak your language!

Keep your luggage in sight throughout the time that you are going through the check in process and also on the journey to your room. Carry any bags containing your passport, travel documents, business papers or laptop yourself.

Once you get to your room, take a moment to see where everything is and that it works. Check for door viewers, chains, bolts. Is there a sign on the door showing fire escape routes (and can you remove it if needed)? Check the telephone works and you know or can see the number to dial for "Reception". Protect your luggage, electronic gear, and other valuables at all times. Don't assume that your property is safe in your hotel room. If you must travel with valuable personal items or documents, ask the hotel manager to keep them in the hotel safe (not the room safe) when you're not using them.

Once you have settled into your room, take some time to look around the hotel and see what facilities are available. Physically check the route from your room to the nearest fire exit and emergency exit stairways. Does the hotel have any CCTV or security guards visible? What about fire extinguishers or sprinklers?

Be wary of any callers at your room door, especially during the night. Always use the door viewer and chain when answering the door. If in doubt, call reception immediately.

Fire alarms can happen at any time, so always have your essential items close to hand whenever you are in your room. If the fire alarm does go off, do not assume it is a “false alarm”. Get your essentials and start to leave immediately.

Chapter 5: Out & About

Apart from the obvious language differences, it can often come as a surprise to travellers just how different other countries can be. Culture, dress, laws, traffic standards, health & safety standards, security levels, availability of cash, goods and services will definitely be different your "home" country. In many countries, these standards may be extremely lower or even non-existent. Good planning conducted prior to your trip should help you to prepare and adapt your travel plans for this, but it is worth highlighting some of the more serious issues that you should consider:

Laws and cultural practice can vary dramatically from country to country. What may seem perfectly acceptable practice in "Western" countries can bring hostility from the public or the risk of prosecution by the local Police. As was mentioned in the section dealing with "preparing for your trip", a great deal of advice regarding this issue can be found on the UK or US government "travel advice" websites.

Additional information can be found in "online" travel guides, such as "lonely planet".

Many countries insist of your carrying government identity documents, such s photo ID Cards or passports at all times. In some countries, photographing locations such as military and police installations, industrial/transport infrastructure and border crossings can lead to the confiscation of the camera and film or penalties, including a fine or even imprisonment. In some (particularly Gulf Arab countries), use of "strong" language, offensive hand gestures or even raising your voice to "locals" can cause you to be arrested, questioned and even convicted of an offence

Attitudes towards sexuality, women and ethnic minority groups may be completely different to your home country. Indeed, in many countries, homosexuality is illegal and the punishments upon conviction will be harsh, including the death penalty. In certain countries, women can attract negative attention simply for dining alone or appearing alone at social gatherings. Observe your hotel restaurant and local dining establishments for clues as to local social norms.

Fake wedding rings can help single women ward off unwanted attention. Avoid eye contact. Some men may view eye contact as a 'come-on'.

Male travellers are also not immune from unwanted attention in bars and other entertainment venues. In many countries, solicitation by "working girls" can be very forthright, bordering on "aggressive". In some countries, those offering their "services" may be working in collusion with criminal gangs, or even the local police, with the intention of "setting up" unwary travellers to incidents of bribery, theft assault or even detention & deportation.

All travellers should be aware of the dangers of drinks being tampered with in bars & restaurants. A close watch should be kept on the way in which drinks are being prepared and served at the bar and they should never be left unattended on tables. Avoid drinking too much, as this will leave you vulnerable. Similarly, becoming too boisterous may drawn unwanted attention from others in the premises or from security staff or the police.

What you wear can either bring unwanted attention or help you blend in. As a general rule, tight and skimpy clothing is inappropriate in most countries outside of Western Europe and North America. Clothing should be conservative, loose fitting, and comfortable. Arms and legs should be covered, especially when visiting places of worship and national monuments. Throughout the Arab world and in other Muslin countries, women's hair is usually covered with a head scarf.

In some countries, some articles of clothing such as "military" style jackets and trousers, or Tee shirts with explicit pictures or wording will be considered offensive and may even be illegal.

Don't forget to wear clothing which is appropriate for the environment, which will help protect you from the sun, or from the local wildlife (mosquitoes).

Try to void wearing clothing displaying company "logos" or nationality "flags" as they will immediately draw attention to you.

Try to keep to the main city streets, especially if travelling alone and especially at night. Jewellery or other expensive fashion accessories should be kept to a minimum and valuables such as wallets and mobile phones should be kept out of sight. Attempt to blend in with the local environment and avoid drawing attention to yourself. Avoid routine patterns and vary travel routes and be conscious of the possibility of being followed. Pay attention to your surroundings and trust your instincts. Leave areas where you feel ill at ease, where there are large crowds gathering or signs of any public protest or disorder.

Try not to be the last person leaving the bar, club or restaurant at the end of the day. When travelling in vehicles, always wear seatbelts and lock the doors from the inside. Similarly, if you are in a taxi, make sure that you can open the window or door from the inside! Don't share a taxi with people you do not know, or with people you may have just met socially. In some countries, it is common for taxis to pick up additional passengers when on route to gain additional "fares". Do not allow your taxi to do this and do not get into a taxi that already has a passenger.

If you do find yourself being questioned by the Police or other state authorities, remain calm and dignified. Always ask to see some form of "ID", even from a policeman in uniform. Try to avoid following them to a quiet area "to talk" or to get into a vehicle with them. If there is a language barrier, make it obvious that you do not understand – keep talking in your own language and mention the words "English", "Embassy" or "Diplomatic". Usually, one of these words will "register" in any language. Show your passport copy, rather than your passport. Do not offer money!

If the situation looks as if it may be more than a "routine ID check", then immediately contact your Embassy for assistance. While remaining polite, do not sign anything before taking advice from your embassy and do not admit or volunteer to anything. Never make jokes about drugs, religion, weapons, bombs or "police harassment" as this will most certainly escalate the situation to the highest level.

Chapter 6: Final thoughts

For most people, travel is a safe and enjoyable experience. However, why "trust to luck", for when things go wrong in a foreign country, what would be a minor inconvenience in your home country can quickly escalate into a major problem, with the potential for possibly severe consequences.

Being prepared before your trip will help you to avoid the more common "mistakes" made by many travellers and provides you with some appropriate solutions if problems do arise.

Hopefully, this guide will help you on your future travels. Should you need any further information on any aspect of personal or business security, particularly for travel to high risk countries, then please visit our website at www.securitymanagementsolutions.co.uk

Have a safe and enjoyable trip!

References

Listed below are some suggestions for websites you may wish to check out when planning for your trip:

UK government travel advice website
www.gov.uk/foreign-travel-advice

US government travel advice website
www.travel.state.gov/travel

Lonely planet online travel guides
www.lonelyplanet.com/

Trip advisor online travel guides
www.tripadvisor.co.uk/TravelGuides

World city guides
www.businesstraveller.com/city-guides

CIA online world fact book
www.ciaworldfactbook.us

World risk map
www.aon.com/2013politicalriskmap

Security advice and services
www.securitymanagementsolutions.co.uk

Example travel itinerary

Travel Itinerary

DAY:		DATE:			
Transfer to airport					
Company:		Reservation #		Pickup Time:	am/pm
Flight					
Depart From:		To:		Flight #:	
Check in time:	am/pm	Depart:	am/pm	Arrive:	am/pm
Transfer from airport					
Company:		Reservation #		Time:	am/pm
Accommodation					
Hotel:		Reservation #		Check-in time:	am/pm
Address:				Phone:	
DAY:		DATE:			
Checkout time:	am/pm				
Transfer to airport					
Company:		Reservation #		Time:	am/pm
Flight					
Depart From:		To:		Flight #:	
Check in time:	am/pm	Depart:	am/pm	Arrive:	am/pm
Transfer from airport					
Company:		Reservation #		Pickup Time:	am/pm
CAR RENTAL:					
Rental Company:		Reservation #			
Pick up date:		time:	am/pm		
Drop off date:		time:	am/pm		
Beginning km:		End km:		Fuel:	$

www.ingramcontent.com/pod-product-compliance
Ingram Content Group UK Ltd.
Pitfield, Milton Keynes, MK11 3LW, UK
UKHW020215250726
13967UKWH00001B/4

9 781291 592030